A Mouse Told His Mother

by Bethany Roberts ★ Illustrated by Maryjane Begin

Visit The Learning Site!
www.harcourtschool.com

This edition is published by special arrangement with Little, Brown and Company (Inc.), New York.

Grateful acknowledgment is made to Little, Brown and Company (Inc.), New York, for permission to reprint *A Mouse Told His Mother* by Bethany Roberts, illustrated by Maryjane Begin.

Printed in China

ISBN 10 0-15-352472-3
ISBN 13 978-0-15-352472-1

2 3 4 5 6 7 8 9 10 985 15 14 13 12 11 10 09 08 07

A Mouse Told His Mother

To my parents, who believed
I could be anything I wanted to be
B. R.

To "The Boys"—Kit, Chuck, and Craig
M. B.

NATURE

A mouse told his mother,
“I am going on a trip.”
“It is bedtime,” said his mother.

A mouse told his mother,
"I am going to the moon."
"Take your toothbrush,"
said his mother.

UNITED STATES

AT
OOD

A mouse told his mother,
"I am off to catch a crocodile."
"Don't forget to wash your feet,"
said his mother.

A mouse told his mother,
"I will dive for pirate treasure."
"You'd better bring a towel,"
said his mother.

A mouse told his mother,
"I will climb up
snowcapped mountains."
"Wear warm pajamas,"
said his mother.

A mouse told his mother,
"I will hop into an airplane
and fly around the world."
"Hop right into bed now,"
said his mother.

A mouse told his mother,
"I will ride a bucking bronco."
"Here's your pillow," said his mother.

A mouse told his mother,
"I'll cross burning desert sands."
"How about a glass of water?"
asked his mother.

A mouse told his mother,
"I'll drive sled dogs through a blizzard."
"You may need an extra blanket,"
said his mother.

A mouse told his mother,
"I'll explore a spooky cave."
"Lights out now," said his mother.

A mouse told his mother,
"I'll tame bears in a circus."
"Here's a bear hug,"
said his mother.

A mouse told his mother,
"I will sail where the wind blows."
"Blow me a kiss," said his mother.

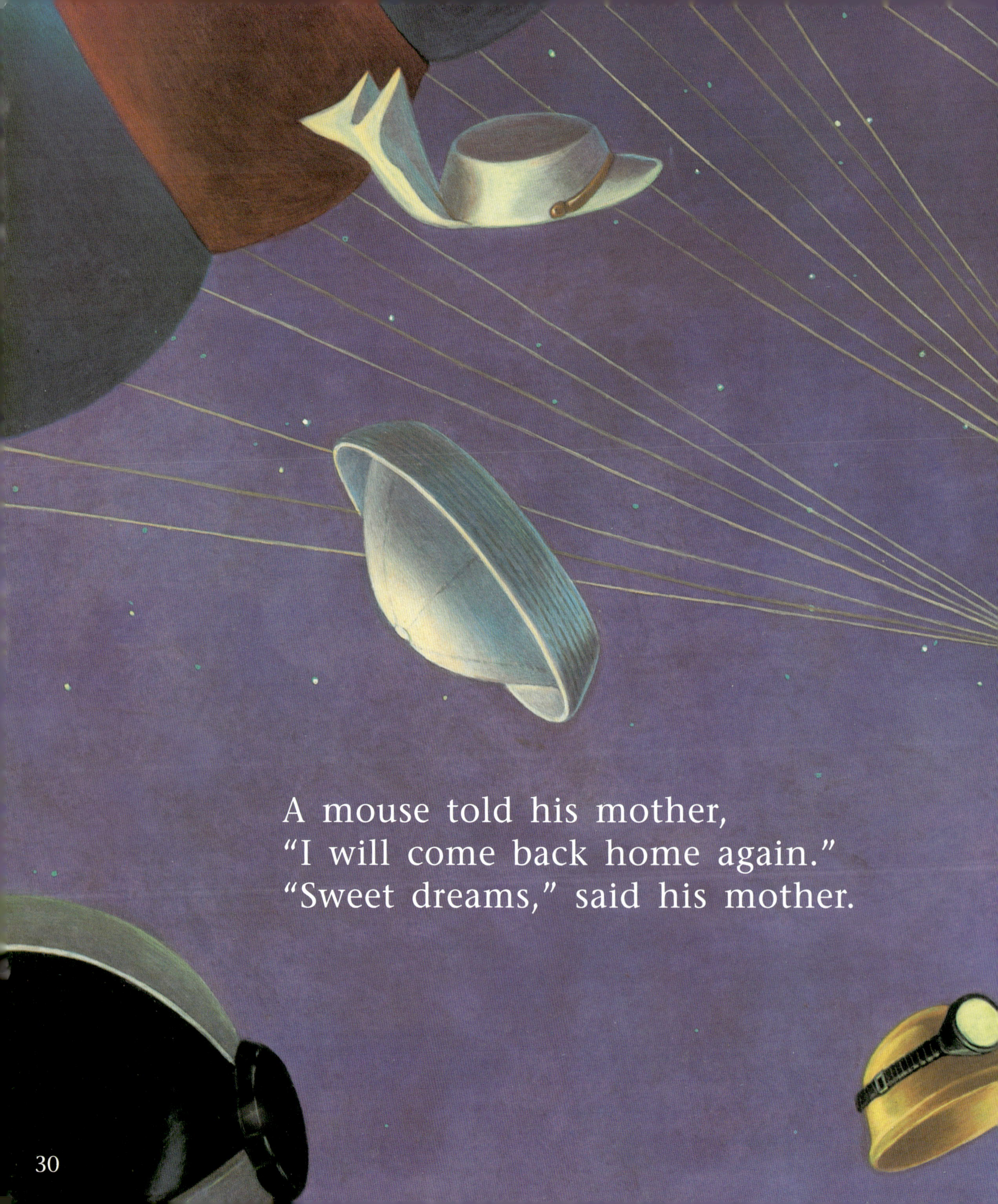

A mouse told his mother,
"I will come back home again."
"Sweet dreams," said his mother.

"And good night."